Bryn Ma~

Euripides'
Bacchae

Beth Causey

Manufactured in the United States of America
ISBN 0-929524-85-3
Printed and distributed by
Bryn Mawr Commentaries
Thomas Library
Bryn Mawr College
101 North Merion Avenue
Bryn Mawr, PA 19010-2899

Series Preface

These lexical and grammatical notes are meant not as a full-scale commentary but as a clear and concise aid to the beginning student. The editors have been told to resist their critical impulses and to say only what will help the student read the text. Our commentaries, then, are the beginning of the interpretive process, not the end.

We expect that the student will know the basic Attic declensions and conjugations, basic grammar (the common functions of cases and moods; the common types of clauses and conditions), and how to use a dictionary. In general we have tried to avoid duplication of material easily extractable from the lexicon, but we have included help with the odd verb forms, and recognizing that endless page-flipping can be counter-productive, we have provided the occasional bonus of assistance with uncommon vocabulary.

These commentaries are based on the Oxford Classical Text unless otherwise noted. Oxford University Press has kindly allowed us to print its edition of the Greek text in cases where we thought it would be particularly beneficial to the student.

Production of these commentaries has been made possible by a generous grant from the Division of Education Programs, the National Endowment for the Humanities.

Richard Hamilton
General Editor

Preface

These notes are meant to help students at the intermediate level who are using E.R. Dodds' Oxford commentary on Euripides' *Bacchae*. They should in no way be viewed as a substitute for his indispensable discussion of the text, for I have included nothing which is readily accessible in his notes. Therefore, I would encourage those using this Supplement always to check Dodds first when encountering difficulty with the text and to turn to my notes only when expeditious assistance is not to be found there. Since Dodds was writing for experts as well as students, potentially helpful comments are often buried within complex scholarly notes and difficult for the intermediate student in search of immediate assistance to locate. On these occasions I have extracted or paraphrased his remarks on the specific textual problems. I have also included in the Supplement Dodds' headings for the different sections of the play (Prologue, Parodos, etc.) in order to alert users of this volume to the excellent introductions he provides at the beginning of each.

I would like to thank Aaron Wolpert and Aileen Ruggles for their valuable contributions to the final editing and Professor Deborah Roberts and the students of her Greek tragedy class at Haverford College for testing this Supplement in the spring of 1994. It was written at Bryn Mawr College with the support of a Dorothy Nepper Marshall Fellowship. I am especially grateful to Professor Gregory Dickerson for his endless patience and invaluable guidance and help.

Metrical Note

Greek meter depends not upon accent or stress, as in English poetry, but upon the amount of time required to pronounce each successive syllable. Syllables are called long (-) or short (˘) based on the vowels and consonants they contain without any regard to accent or stress. ε and o are short vowels, ω and η, and all diphthongs, are long, and α, ι, and υ may be either long or short. One can determine whether one of the last three is long or short by checking the lexicon for a macron or circumflex over the letter in question, or by what is necessary for the meter. The letters following a vowel, whether in the same word or the following word, can influence whether the syllable is long or short.

A syllable is <u>long</u> if it contains:

1) a long vowel or diphthong.

2) a short vowel followed by a double consonant (ξ, ζ, ψ).

3) a short vowel followed by more than one consonant, EXCEPT when the first is a mute (β, γ, δ, θ, κ, π, τ, φ, and χ, i.e., all consonants except the liquids and σ) and the second is a liquid (μ, ν, λ, ρ). This is called the "mute-liquid rule" ("Attic correption"), which states that if a short vowel is followed by two consonants, a mute and a liquid, the syllable will in most cases remain short. However, this is not a hard and fast rule and there are often exceptions necessitated by the meter.

A syllable is <u>short</u> if it contains:

1) a short vowel not followed by a consonant.

2) a short vowel followed by one consonant which is not a double consonant.

3) a short vowel followed by two consonants which fall under the mute-liquid rule.

In tragedy, most narrative and dialogue outside of the choruses is written in iambic trimeter, so called because, in its "pure" form, the line contains three metra, each containing two iambic feet: ˘ - ˘ - | ˘ - ˘ - | ˘ - ˘ -. In practice, there is considerable room for the poet to vary this pattern by substituting long for short syllables in the first, third, and fifth feet, or a short for a long syllable in the final foot of the line. A syllable which may be either short or long (called an "anceps") is marked by x. Thus, the standard scansion of the iambic trimeter can be schematized as follows:

x - ˘ - | x - ˘ - | x - ˘ x.

Often, Euripides uses two short syllables to stand in place of one long syllable. This is called resolution, and it can occur either in the anceps positions or in those which require a long syllable.

Lines 10-11 of the *Bacchae* provide a helpful illustration of some of the variation which is possible within the pattern of the iambic trimeter.

＿ ＿ ◡ ＿ | ◡ ◡ ◡ ◡ ＿ | ◡ ＿ ◡ ◡

αἰνῶ δὲ Κάδμον, ἄβατον ὃς πέδον τόδε

◡ ＿ ◡ ◡ ◡ | ＿ ＿ ＿ ◡ ＿ | ◡ ＿ ◡ ◡

τίθησι, θυγατρὸς σηκόν· ἀμπέλου δέ νιν

In the first of these lines, Euripides substitutes a long for a short syllable only once, at the very beginning, while at the same time "resolving" the long syllable at the end of the first foot of the second metron into two short syllables (ἄβα-), producing the pattern ◡ ◡ ◡ where we expect ◡ ＿ or ＿ ＿. In the following line, he has used an identical resolution as a substitute for a simple iamb at the end of the first metron, producing the pattern ◡ ◡ ◡ (-σι, θυγα-) where we expect ◡ ＿. Note that scansion of this line reveals that the second syllable of θυǀγαǀτρός must be short, an example of the "mute-liquid rule" at work.

The meters of the choruses, which are more various and complex than iambic trimeter, are thoroughly analyzed by Dodds in his commentary.

Commentary

Abbreviations:

D   E. R. Dodds, *Euripides, Bacchae*, (Oxford 1960)

GP   J. D. Denniston, *The Greek Particles*[2] (Oxford 1954)

S   H. W. Smyth, *Greek Grammar*, rev. by G. M. Messing (Cambridge, Mass. 1956)

Prologue

1   τήνδε ... χθόνα: "to this land"; terminal acc. In poetry, the goal of a verb of motion is often in acc. without a preposition (S 1588).

3   λοχευθεῖσ(α) < λοχεύω, "to bring to birth."

4   ἀμείψας ἐκ: "having taken x (acc.) in exchange for y (gen.)."

7   τόδ(ε): "this one here," indicating, as often, someone or something present on stage.

9   μητέρ(α) εἰς ἐμήν: "against my mother." In poetry an object can precede its preposition.

     ἀθάνατον ... ὕβριν: in apposition to φλόγα.

11   τίθησι: "establish x (acc.) as y (acc. adj.)."

     σηκόν: "shrine."

     νιν: third person, sing. or pl., masc. or fem. accusative pronoun used frequently in poetry (S 325e). Here, masc. acc. sing.

11f ἀμπέλου ... βοτρυώδει χλόῃ: "with the clustered greenery of the grape-vine."

13 γύας < γύης, ου, ὁ, "field, land."

14f Φρυγῶν τε, Περσῶν θ': The first τε connects Λυδῶν in 13 and Φρυγῶν. θ' connects the phrase governed by ἐπελθών in line 16 to the phrase governed by λιπών in line 13. The comma shows the point after which the acc.'s are objects of ἐπελθών rather than λιπών. The remaining connectives link the objects of ἐπελθών.

14 πλάκας < πλάξ, πλακός, ἡ, "plain, plateau."

17 ἅλα < ἅλς, ἁλός, ἡ, "sea," as in Homer.

18 μιγάσιν < μιγάς, άδος, "mixed, mingled."

19 πλήρεις < πλήρης, ες, "filled (with)," here + preceding dat.'s.

     καλλιπυργώτους: "with beautiful towers."

20 D believes that this line should follow line 22, but if it remains in this position, he suggests substituting χθόνα for πόλιν to avoid repetition after πόλεις in 19.

21 τἀκεῖ = τὰ ἐκεῖ, "the regions there." D prefers (in combination with his shift of line 20) κἀκεῖ = καὶ ἐκεῖ, which is the reading of the manuscripts.

22 τελετάς: "rites," especially of initiation.

24 ἀνωλόλυξα < ἀνολολύζω, here causal "excite with cries."

     νεβρίδ(α) < νεβρίς, ίδος, ἡ, "fawnskin."

     ἐξάψας < ἐξάπτω, "to fasten x (acc.) to y (gen.)."

     χροός < χρώς, χροός, ὁ, "skin, flesh, body."

26   ἃς ἥκιστα χρῆν: "for whom it was least necessary." χρῆν = unaugmented imperfect of χρῆ.

27   οὐκ ἔφασκον: "denied."

28   νυμφευθεῖσαν < νυμφεύω, literally, "give in marriage."
ἐκ: a common poetic alternative to ὑπό + gen. as an expression of personal agent (S 1688c).

29   ἀναφέρειν: "attribute"; continues indirect statement introduced by οὐκ ἔφασκον in 27 but without the negative.

30   Κάδμου σοφίσμα(τα): "a wily strategem belonging to Kadmos." In Greek poetry, the plural is often used where English uses an indefinite singular (S 1000b). As D points out, the phrase is in apposition to Semele's claim that Zeus is the father of her baby (Σεμέλην ... ἀναφέρειν), which her sisters dismiss as a face-saving expedient devised by their father Kadmos.
νιν = αὐτήν, i.e., Semele; see on 11.

31   ἐξεκαυχῶν(το) < ἐκκαυχάομαι, "gloatingly announce." This is an ἅπαξ λεγόμενον, the only occurrence of this compound verb.
γάμους: here, her affair with Zeus.

32   νιν: here, fem. pl., intensified by αὐτάς.
ᾠστρησ(α) < οἰστράω, "goad."

33   φρενῶν: For the gen. of separation, see S 1392; here, dependent on παράκοποι, "struck aside from."

35f πᾶν ... ἦσαν: As punctuated in the text, these lines seem to say the same thing twice, perhaps to stress the exclusion of males from maenadic ritual. For an alternative punctuation which removes the tautology and produces a more normal iambic line, see D.

36   ἐξέμηνα < ἐκμαίνω, "drive mad."

37   ἀναμεμειγμέναι < ἀναμίγνυμι/ἀναμίσγω, "mix up, mix together."

38   ἀνορόφοις ... πέτραις: literally, "on roofless rocks." In poetry, the dat. of place is often expressed without a preposition (S 1531).
ἧνται < ἧμαι, "sit"; for the conjugation, see S 789.

40   ἀτέλεστον οὖσαν: participle in indirect statement with ἐκμαθεῖν in 39.
βακχευμάτων: with ἀτέλεστον, "uninitiated"; see on 33.

41   Σεμέλης ... ὕπερ: The accent on a disyllabic preposition shifts to the first syllable (anastrophe) when its object precedes it (S 175).

42   τίκτει: Subject is Semele.

45   τὰ κατ' ἐμέ: literally, "the (actions) involving me"; internal acc. (S 1554a) with θεομαχεῖ.
ἄπο: For accent, see on 41.

47   αὐτῷ ... γεγὼς ἐνδείξομαι (< ἐνδείκνυμαι): "show, give proof of being x (participle) to y (dat.)."

50   ἢν = ἐάν.

52   μαινάσι < μαινάς, άδος, ἡ, "madwoman, Bacchante."

53   ἀλλάξας (< ἀλλάσσω) ἔχω: "I have taken in exchange." ἔχω + aor. part. = periphrastic perfect (S 599b).

5 5 ἔρυμα < ἔρυμα, ατος, τό, "defence, bulwark."

5 8 τἀπιχώρι(α) = τὰ ἐπιχώρια, "native."

5 9 ἐμά: The possessive adj. is often substituted for a parallel possessive pronoun, here ἐμοῦ.

6 1 κτυπεῖτε: causal, "make (them, i.e., the τύμπανα) resound."

6 3 ἵν(α): "where," as usual when followed by the indicative.

Parodos

6 4 γᾶς = γῆς. In tragic choruses Doric α is often substituted for Attic η.

6 7 κάματόν τ' εὐκάματον: literally, "toil easily toiled."

6 8 εὐαζομένα = εὐαζομένη; see on 64.

6 9 τίς;: D's commentary is based on Gilbert Murray's edition of the text, with which he frequently disagrees. Here, objecting to Murray's monosyllabic question, he prefers the reading τίς μελάθροις ("Who (is) in the house?"). For dat. of place, see on 38.

     εὔφημον: "uttering words of good omen" here, as often, implies, in order to avoid bad omens, uttering no words at all, i.e., to observe religious silence.

7 2 ὑμνήσω: "sing, praise, celebrate," takes double acc. of the thing praised and the thing wherein or with which it is praised.

7 4 βιοτὰν ἁγιστεύει: literally, "keeps pure with respect to his life."

7 5 θιασεύεται: literally, "bring into the θίασος/Bacchic company."

7 6 ὄρεσσι < ὄρος, ὄρους, τό, "hill," Homeric dat.

7 8 ὄργια: "worship, rites, sacrifices," especially those practiced secretly by the initiated.

7 9 θεμιτεύων: "practicing according to the rite fixed by θέμις (religious law)."

8 0 ἀνά ... τινάσσων: As D points out, tmesis of ἀνατινάσσω, "shake up and down, brandish." For tmesis, see S 1650-1651.

8 7 ἀγυιάς < ἀγυιά, ᾶς, ἡ, "street, highway."

8 8 ὠδίνων < ὠδίς, ῖνος, ἡ, "travail, labor pain."

8 9 λοχίαις: "of childbirth, natal."

9 0 πταμένας < πέτομαι, "fly," aor. mid. part.; gen. absolute, as D explains.

     νηδύος < νηδύς, ύος, ἡ, "stomach, womb"; gen. of separation with ἔκβολον, "cast from, aborted."

9 7 συνερείδει < συνερείδω, "set firmly together, bind closely."

9 9 ἀνίκα = ἡνίκα, "when."

1 0 0 ταυρόκερων: masc. acc. sing., "bull-horned." For the accent, see S 163a.

100f τέλεσαν ... στεφάνοσεν: For the omission of the syllabic past indicative augment in Attic tragedy, see S 438a.

1 0 2 ἔνθεν: "from which cause"(D).

     θηροτρόφον: literally, "beast-fed," i.e., "bestial, wild."

1 0 4 πλοκάμοις: "locks, braids of hair."

1 0 6 κισσῷ: "ivy."

109   **καταβακχιοῦσθε:** literally, "make yourselves thoroughly Bacchantes."
111   **ἐνδυτά:** "garments."
112   **λευκοτρίχων ... μαλλοῖς:** literally, "with wool of white-haired curls." λευκοτρίχων < λευκόθριξ, λευκότριχος.
113   **ἀμφί:** here + acc., "concerning." **νάρθηκας** < νάρθηξ, ηκος, ἡ, "cane, fennel rod." In the *Bacchae*, νάρθηξ = θύρσος.
114f   Murray's text of this line, which in 115 substitutes ὅστις for the ὅτε found in both manuscripts and adds dashes to produce a parenthetical statement, would be translated, "—(and) he is the Roarer (the god Dionysos), whoever leads the θίασοι—." This reading led to the belief that Dionysos took over the identity of the human leader of the maenads. Murray's reading and its implications have been persuasively refuted by more recent scholarship, which joins D in preferring εὖτ' ἄν, "whenever," as the required emendation. (The ὅτε of the manuscripts does not fit the meter, and the subjunctive ἄγῃ justifies the need for ἄν.) D's changes produce a smooth sentence which fits the context: "At once the whole earth will dance whenever the Roarer leads the θίασοι ..." Dionysos leads the maenads himself rather than entering into the body of a male leader.
119   **Διονύσῳ:** a rare use of the dat. of personal agent with a tense of the passive other than perfect or pluperfect (S 1490).
121   **ζάθεοι:** "exceedingly holy." The prefix δα- or ζα- intensifies the word to which it is attached (S 885.8).
123   To clarify the syntax and avoid interlinear hiatus, D prefers to read τρικόρυθες ἔνθ' ἐν ἄντροις.
124   **βυρσότονον κύκλωμα:** "circle with stretched hide," i.e., a drum.
127   **κέρασαν** < κεράννυμι, "mix, mingle." For the lack of augment, see on 100.
       ἀδυβόᾳ: Doric dat. < ἡδυβόης, ου, "sweet-sounding."
129   **εὐάσμασι** < εὔασμα, ατος, τό, "cry of εὐοῖ," i.e., "a Bacchanalian shout."
       βακχᾶν: Doric gen. pl.; see S215 D8.
130   **παρά:** governs ματέρος.
131   **ἐξανύσαντο** < ἐξανύω, middle, "obtain"; sc. τύμπανα as object. For the lack of augment see on 100.
       ματέρος = μητέρος.
133   **τριετηρίδων** < τριετηρίς, ίδος, ἡ, literally, "triennial festival."
135f   **ἡδὺς ... Βρόμιος:** As at 114f., the text here is important for understanding maenadic ritual. Murray's text, which D defends in the main body of his note, follows the reading of the major manuscripts (ὅταν), and assumes that Dionysos is the subject of the sentence: "He (the god) is welcome in the hills *whenever* he falls ..., and our leader is the Roarer (140)." This is the text and interpretation preferred by most recent scholarship, eliminating any reference to a male mortal as leader of the group. D rejects this reading in footnote 2 at the bottom of the

same page (86), in favor of emending ὅταν to ὃς ἄν: "He is pleasing in the hills *whoever* falls ..., and (he,) our cult leader is/becomes the Roarer." This contradicts his preferred reading of 114 and reintroduces into the text the idea of a temporarily deified male cult leader.

139 ἱέμενος < ἵημι, middle, "send oneself, hasten."
142 μελισσᾶν: "of bees"; see on 129.
144 λιβάνου: "frankincense."
147 ἀίσσει: "sets in motion (transitive); moves quickly, darts (intransitive)." Here, transitive; obj. is φλόγα.
151 ἐπιβρέμει: "roars out."
153 [ᾧ]: Square brackets are used to indicate words which the editor (here, Murray) believes should be removed from the text as erroneous interpolations by someone other than the author.
154 χρυσορόου: "with streams of gold."
χλιδᾷ < χλιδή, ῆς, ἡ, "luxury, costly ornament," here, perhaps castanets. D, troubled by the vagueness of the instrument to which the dative refers, prefers to emend to the vocative, χλιδά.
155 μέλπετε: "celebrate with song and dance."
158 εὔια τὸν εὔιον ἀγαλλόμεναι θεόν: "exalting with Bacchic cries the god of the Bacchic cry"; εὔια: internal acc. with ἀγαλλόμεναι.
161 σύνοχα: "in accord with, in company with," + dat.
162 φοιτάσιν < φοιτάς, άδος, "roaming wildly."
166 πῶλος ὅπως: "like a foal." In tragedy, postpositive ὅπως often substitutes for ὡς in introducing comparisons (S 2463).
167 φορβάδι < φορβάς, άδος, "grazing, feeding."
σκιρτήμασι < σκίρτημα, ατος, τό, "leap."
Βάκχα: modified by ἡδομένα in 165.

Scene 1

170 ἐκκάλει: imperative, as the accent shows.
176 νεβρῶν δοράς: "skins of fawns."
177 βλαστήμασιν: "shoots, sprouts."
178f ὡς σὴν γῆρυν ἠσθόμην κλύων σοφὴν σοφοῦ παρ' ἀνδρός: literally, "for I perceived your voice, hearing it as wise from a wise man."
182 For the square brackets, see on 153. D thinks Murray's reasons for deleting this line are "not conclusive."
183 ὅσον καθ' ἡμᾶς δυνατόν: "as much as (is) possible, as far as we are concerned."
187 κάμοιμ(ι): 2nd aor. < κάμνω, here, "be weary."
188 ἐπιλελήσμεθ(α) < ἐπιλανθάνομαι, "forget," with supplementary participle in indirect discourse (S 2106).
189 ταῦτ(α) = τὰ αὐτά, crasis (S 68).
ἐμοί: "as I" (S 1500).
190 ἡβῶ < ἡβάω, "be young, be in the prime of youth."

κἀπιχειρήσω = καὶ ἐπιχειρήσω < ἐπιχειρέω, "put one's hand to, make an attempt."

191 **περάσομεν** < περάω, "cross, traverse, pass."

194 **ἀμοχθί:** "without toil, easily."

νῷν: 1st person dual dat.

196 **γάρ:** "yes, for ...," as often in answer to a question (GP 73).

197 **τὸ μέλλειν:** "being about to (do something), delay, hesitation."

ἔχου < ἔχομαι + gen, "grasp, hold on to." For the gen. with verbs of touching and holding, see S 1345.

198 **ἰδού:** so accented, an adverb calling attention to what is taking place, "there!"

ξυνωρίζου < συνωρίζω, "yoke together like a pair of horses, join."

199 **καταφρονῶ:** "look down on, think contemptuously of," + gen.

200 **οὐδὲν σοφιζόμεσθα:** -μεσθα = -μεθα; D prefers οὐδ' ἐνσοφιζόμεσθα: "Nor do we use cleverness on." With this correction, he gives the line to Kadmos, but the change to first person plural from singular in 199 is so jarring that he thinks at least one line may have been lost.

202 **κεκτήμεθ(α)** < κτάομαι, "acquire."

αὐτά: antecedent seems to be παραδοχάς, although the pronoun is neuter plural. D thinks there may be something missing.

203 **δι(ά):** + gen. here, "by means of."

206 **διήρηχ'** = διήρεκ(ε), perf. < διαιρέω, "distinguish."

209 **διαριθμῶν δ' οὐδέν':** D prefers δι' ἀριθμῶν οὐδέν, "not at all through units," i. e., "in no way by individuals."

210 **φέγγος:** "light."

211 **προφήτης σοι λόγων:** "interpreter to you in words (of what is happening)" (D).

214 **ἐπτόηται:** perf. < πτοέω, literally, "be all in a flutter."

216 **νεοχμά** = νέα.

πτόλιν = πόλιν.

κακά: The evils are described in the acc.-inf. constructions which follow (216-225).

218 **δασκίοις:** "thick-shaded"; for the prefix δα-, see on 121.

222 **ἄλλην δ' ἄλλοσ(ε):** literally, "another in another direction," i.e., "one in one direction, one in another." For ἄλλος, ἄλλη, ἄλλο repeated in different cases, see S 1274.

224 **πρόφασιν:** "with regard to pretext, ostensibly"; for this sort of adverbial acc., see S 993.

225 **πρόσθε:** + gen., "before."

ἄγειν: here, literally, "treat, hold."

231 **σιδηραῖς ... ἄρκυσιν:** "in iron nets."

232 **κακούργου τῆσδε βακχείας:** gen. of separation with παύω.

235 **εὐοσμῶν κόμην:** literally, "being fragrant with respect to his hair." D prefers to emend κόμην to κομῶν < κομάω, "to wear long hair" and retain εὔοσμον from the manuscripts as an internal acc.

238 νεάνισιν < νεᾶνις, ιδος, ἡ, "girl."

241 τεμών: 2nd aor. part. < τέμνω, "cut."

243 ἐρρᾶφθαι: perf. pass. inf. < ῥάπτω, "stitch, sew."

245 Δίους < Δῖος, adjectival form of Ζεύς.
ὅτι: "because."

248 τόδ(ε): See on 7.

250 γέλων: poetic acc. < γέλως, γέλωτος, ὁ, "laugh, matter for laughter."

251 ἀναίνομαι: literally, "I am ashamed."

253 οὐκ ἀποτινάξεις ...;: "Will you not shake off...?" Here, as often, the negative future question is equivalent to a positive command (S 1918).

254 μεθήσεις < μεθίημι, "let go."

255 θέλεις = ἐθέλεις.

257 κἀμπύρων = καὶ ἐμπύρων, "burnt sacrifices."
μισθοὺς φέρειν: "receive wages." Seers were paid to interpret signs from birds and burnt offerings.

258 ἐξερρύετο < ἐκρύομαι, "protect." ρ is doubled after the past indicative augment (S 429).

259 καθῆσ(ο): imperf. < κάθημαι, "sit."

263 τῆς δυσσεβείας ... θεούς: As printed by Murray, an exclamatory gen., but, as D points out, this construction is not to be found in tragedy without an interjection. δυσσεβείας, or perhaps θεούς, may be corrupt. D speculates that something may have been lost, but prefers τῆς Εὐσεβείας ... θρόνους, "the majesty of Religion," or literally, "the thrones of Reverence," to the text as printed.

264 γηγενῆ στάχυν: "earth-born crop/offspring," obj. of σπείραντα.

268 εὔτροχον: "well-wheeled"; i.e., "quick, glib."

270 θράσει δὲ δύνατος καὶ λέγειν οἷός τ' ἀνήρ: literally, "a man powerful in his rashness and able to speak."

273 μέγεθος: neut. acc., "greatness, magnitude."

276 κάλει: imperative; see on 170.

277 ξηροῖσιν: "the dry"; for the adjective without an article as a noun with general sense, see S 1130.

278 ἀντίπαλον: literally, "as a rival, in opposition."

281 πλησθῶσιν: aor. pass. < πίμπλημι, "fill (with)," + gen.

282 τε: connects παύει in 280 with δίδωσιν in 283.
λήθην: "forgetfulness," in apposition to ὕπνον.

286 ἐνερράφη: aor. pass. < ἐνράπτω, "sew, stitch in."

287 καλῶς ἔχει: ἔχω + adv. = εἰμί + adj. (S 1438).

289 βρέφος < βρέφος, ους, τό, "babe, fetus."

292 ῥήξας: 1st aor. < ῥήγνυμι, "break."

293 ὅμηρον: "hostage."

293f Clearly there is a lacuna here. It is difficult to make sense of the text as it stands. D's translation at the beginning of his note on 292-4 includes his speculation as to what is missing.

294 νεικέων: literally, "quarrels, squabbles."

295 ῥαφῆναι: aor. pass.; see on 243.
300 πολύς: "much," i.e., "in full force."
301 τὸ μέλλον: "the thing about to be; cf. 197.
         μεμηνότας < μαίνομαι, "be mad." Perf. act. has pres. sense.
302 μεταλαβὼν ἔχει: here, "he has laid claim to." For the
         periphrastic perf., see on 53.
304 θιγεῖν: 2nd aor. < θιγγάνω, "touch, take hold of," + gen.
307 πηδῶντα < πηδάω, "leap."
309 μέγαν τ(ε): τε connects μέγαν with πεδῶντα in 307.
310ff μὴ ... αὔχει ... μηδ' ... δόκει: imperatives, governing acc.-inf.
         indirect discourse. Literally, "Don't declare that ..., and don't think that
         ..."
315 ἐς: here, "in relation to."
316 If this line is to be kept, D thinks it is best to read εἰ instead of ἐν in
         315: "But whether moderation in all things exists in nature always, this
         it is necessary to consider." However, if 316 is deleted, he prefers the
         punctuation, ἀλλ' ἐν τῇ φύσει τοῦτο· σκοπεῖν χρή: "But this
         (σωφρονεῖν) is in nature; it is necessary to keep an eye out."
318 διαφθαρήσεται: fut. pass. < διαφθείρω, "corrupt, ruin."
319 ἐφεστῶσιν: perf. subj. < ἐφίστημι, "stand by, near."
323 ἐρεψόμεσθα < ἐρέφω, "cover; crown oneself (middle)"; for -μεσθα,
         see on 200.
324 ξυνωρίς: "yoked pair." Cf. 198.
327 ἄκη < ἄκος, ἄκους, τό, "cure."
332 φρονῶν οὐδὲν φρονεῖς: "(although) using your intelligence, you
         are not at all intelligent."
338 ἐθρέψατο < τρέφω, "rear, nurture."
340 'Αρτέμιδος: For the gen. of comparison, see S 1431.
341 ὃ μὴ πάθῃς σύ: "And don't you suffer this." In sense, the relative
         clause is a coordinate clause; ὅ = καὶ τοῦτο (S 2490).
343 οὐ μὴ προσοίσεις: See on 253. Here the double negative of the
         question is equivalent to a negative imperative.
344 ἐξομόρξῃ: fut. mid. < ἐξομόργνυμι, "wipe off x (acc.) onto y
         (dat.)."
346 μέτειμι < μετά + εἶμι with future sense, as often for εἶμι. δίκην is
         internal acc., "go after/pursue for prosecution."
         ὡς τάχος = ὡς τάχιστα.
347 θάκους < θᾶκος, ου, ὁ "seat, chair of office."
         ἵν(α): "where." See on 63.
348 μοχλοῖς: "crowbars."
         τριαίνου: imperative < τριαινόω, "heave up, overthrow."
349 ἄνω κάτω: "to and fro, topsy-turvy, upside down"; more
         commonly ἄνω καὶ κάτω.
         συγχέας: aor. part. < συγχέω, literally, "pour together," i.e.,
         "demolish, confound."
350 θυέλλαισιν: "stormblasts."
         μέθες: See on 254.

351 δήξομαι: fut. < δάκνω, "bite, sting."
354 λυμαίνεται: "outrage, mistreat."
356 ὡς ἄν: For ἄν with the subjunctive within a purpose clause in poetry, see S 2201a.
358 ὡς: exclamatory.
　　 ποῦ ποτ' εἶ λόγων: "wherever you are in your words," i.e., "what you are saying," a common expression in tragedy.
359 μέμηνας: See on 301.
　　 πρίν: adverbial, "before, earlier."
364 πειρῶ: mid. imperative < πειράω, "try."
365 γέροντε: dual acc.
367 ὅπως: For the independent object clause of effort expressing an urgent exhortation, "See to it that ...," see S 2213.

Stasimon 1

374 ἀίεις < ἀίω, "hear, listen to."
375 ἐς: "against."
379 θιασεύειν: See on 75. This infinitive, γελάσαι in 380, and ἀποπαῦσαι in 381 are in apposition to τάδ' in 378.
381 μερίμνας: "cares."
384 θαλίαις: "festivities."
386 ἀχαλίνων: "unbridled."
391 ἀσάλευτον: "tranquil, unagitated."
392 πόρσω = πρόσω, "far away."
395f With the punctuation as it stands in the text, τε connects the articular inf., τὸ ... φρονεῖν, with τὸ σοφόν as the compound subject of a sentence with ἐστί understood and σοφία as predicate. D prefers to place the period after σοφιά, making the articular infinitive the subject of a new sentence with ἐστί understood, whose predicate is βραχὺς αἰών.
397 ἐπὶ τούτῳ: literally, "on this condition."
398f τις ... φέροι: D prefers to read τίς and to add a question mark after φέροι, believing the word order suggests a question: "Who would not put up with ...?"
401 κακοβούλων: "ill-advised."
　　 φωτῶν < φώς, φωτός, ὁ, "man."
402 ποτί: Doric for πρός.
406 ἄν = ἤν.
409 καλλιστευομένα: "being the most beautiful."
411 κλιτύς < κλιτύς, ύος, ἡ, "slope, hillside."
413 πρόβακχ(ε): "leader of the Bacchae." The word is not to be found in the lexica since it is the product of scholarly conjecture and is not found elsewhere in Greek literature.
　　 εὔιε: See on 158.
416 ὀργιάζειν: "to practice secret rites"; see on ὄργια 78.
424 ᾧ μὴ ταῦτα μέλει: literally, "the one for whom these things are not a care."

10 Euripides' *Bacchae*

425 κατὰ φάος: "during daylight."
426 διαζῆν: inf. < διαζάω, "live, pass through life"; for the conjugation, see S 395.
427 πραπίδα < πραπίς, ίδος, ἡ, "midriff; mind, heart."
429 περισσῶν: "extraordinary, excessive."
431 τὸ φαυλότερον: modifies τὸ πλῆθος in 430.
χρῆται < χράομαι, "experience, make use of." For the conjugation, see S 395.

Scene 2

435 ἄκραν(τα): adverbial neut. pl. "without accomplishing, in vain."
436 ὁ θὴρ δ' ὅδ' ἡμὶν πρᾶος: literally, "this beast for us (was) tame."
437 πόδ(α): acc. sing. "foot."
438 ἤλλαξεν < ἀλλάττω, "change," here referring to color.
γένυν < γένυς, υος, ἡ, "jaw, cheek."
439 δεῖν < δέω, "bind."
ἐφίετο < ἐφίημι, "order, instruct."
441 αἰδοῦς < αἰδώς, οῦς, ἡ, "shame, embarrassment."
443 εἷρξας: aor. < εἵργω, "shut in."
444 κἄδησας = καὶ ἔδησας, < δέω, "bind."
πανδήμου στέγης: See D on 227.
445 φροῦδαι: "gone away, vanished."
446 σκιρτῶσι < σκιρτάω, "leap"; cf. on 167.
448 κλῇδες: "bars, bolts."
ἀνῆκαν: aor. < ἀνίημι, here, "open."
θύρετρ(α): neut. pl., "doors."
450 τἄλλα: "the other things, the remainder," subject of μέλειν.
452 ὠκύς: "swift."
454 ἐφ' ὅπερ: "with a view to which very thing."
455 ταναός "long."
456 παρ': "alongside."
κεχυμένος < χέω, "pour, stream."
461 οὐ κόμπος οὐδείς: "There is no boast." D believes ὄκνος should be substituted for κόμπος: "there is no reluctance." This is a more logical answer to Pentheus' request.
466 εἰσέβησ(ε): causal 1st aor. < εἰσβαίνω, "make (someone) enter."
468 ζεύξας < ζεύγνυμι, "yoke," a common metaphor for marriage. D prefers to read ἐνθάδ' ἔζευξεν.
470 ὁρῶν ὁρῶντα: literally, "seeing (he compelled me) seeing (him)."
472 ἄρρητ(α): "unspeakable," i.e., "forbidden."
476 ἀσκοῦντ(α): masc. sing. acc. part. < ἀσκέω, "practice"; sc. τινα.
ὄργι(α): subject.
478 'τασσον = ἔτασσον, "I was (not) prescribing."
479 τοῦτ' αὖ παρωχέτευσας εὖ κοὐδὲν λέγων: literally, "Again you diverted this well and by saying nothing."
480 ἀμαθεῖ: dat. sing, < ἀμαθής, ές, "ignorant."

486 σεμνότητ(α) < σεμνότης, "solemnity."
487 σαθρόν: "rotten."
488 κἄν = καὶ ἐν.
489 δίκην ... δοῦναι: "to pay the penalty."
      σοφισμάτων κακῶν: "evil contrivances"; for the gen. of the
      crime, see S 1375.
490 Supply δίκην δοῦναι δεῖ from the previous line.
492 εἴφ' = εἰπέ; for the change in accent, see S 174.
      τί με τὸ δεινὸν ἐργάσῃ: ἐργάζομαι takes two acc.'s; literally,
      "As what will you do this terrible thing to me?" a common way to say
      in Greek, "What is this terrible thing you will do to me?"
493 ἁβρὸν βόστρυχον: literally, "luxurious lock."
      τεμῶ: fut. < τέμνω; see on 241.
495 παράδος: imperative < παραδίδωμι, "hand over."
      χεροῖν: dual gen., "hands."
496 μ(ε) ἀφαιροῦ: mid. imperative < ἀφαιρέω, here with two acc.'s,
      one of which is understood; "take (the thyrsos) away from me."
497 εἱρκταῖσι: here, "prison."
500 πλησίον: "nearby."
503 λάζυσθε: imperative < λάζυμαι, "seize."
      καταφρονεῖ: See on 199; here a rare usage + acc.
504 μὴ δεῖν: μή is the negative used with an infinitive standing for an
      imperative in indirect discourse; for δεῖν, see on 439.
      σώφροσιν: dat. pl. < σώφρων; sc. ὑμῖν.
506 ὅ τι ζῆς: D prefers <ἔθ'> ὅ τι φῇς: "(you no longer know) what you
      are saying."
510 ὡς ἄν: See on 356.
      κνέφας: neut. acc., "darkness."
513 δούπου ... κτύπου: "this thumping and noise of the hide (i.e.,
      drum)."
514 δμωίδας < δμωΐς, ίδος, ἡ, "female slave."
      κεκτήσομαι: fut. perf., "shall have acquired, shall possess"; see on
      202.
517 μέτεισι: See on 346.
518 ἀδικῶν: part. < ἀδικέω, "do wrong."
      κεῖνον = ἐκεῖνον.

Stasimon 2

521 παγαῖς: "running water, streams."
527 βᾶθι = βῆθι. 2nd aor. imperative < βαίνω.
      νηδύν: See on 90; here a terminal acc (see on 1).
531 ἀπωθῇ: mid. < ἀποθέω, "push away from oneself."
532 ἔχουσαν: agrees with με in 530. The chorus refers to itself as
      female.
533 ἀναίνῃ < ἀναίνομαι, here transitive, "reject"; cf. the intransitive use
      in 251.

534f ναὶ τὰν βοτρυώδη Διονύσου χάριν οἴνας: "Indeed, by the grape-clustered charm of the vine of Dionysos"; for ναί + acc. in affirmative oaths, see S 1596b.

536 μελήσει: impersonal, "there will be a care for (someone—dat.) for (something—gen.)."

537 οἵαν οἵαν: D prefers to omit this line, to which nothing corresponds in the strophe. If it is retained, it is exclamatory.

542 ἀγριωπὸν τέρας: "wild-faced monster/marvel."

544 ἀντίπαλον: See on 278.

545 βρόχοισι: "nets, snares."

552 ἀμίλλαισιν: literally, "contests, conflicts."

553 μόλε: aor. imperative < βλώσκω, "come, go."

556 πόθι = ποῦ.

568 ὠκυρόαν: "swift-flowing."

569 εἰλισσομένας = ἑλισσομένας < ἑλίσσομαι, "turn around, spin."

571 τε: D points out that this τε is problematic. It may simply link the two named rivers, the Axios and the Lydios, although its position suggests the addition of a third, unnamed river.

573 τόν: For the article acting as a rel. pron., see S 1105. Its antecedent is the river, and it acts as the subject of λιπαίνειν, "enrich," in indirect discourse after a verb of perceiving (ἔκλυον).

578f τίς ὅδε, τίς <ὅδε> πόθεν ὁ κέλαδος ἀνά μ' ἐκάλεσεν: As punctuated in the text,"What (is) this cry, what (and) from where. (which) summoned me?" Greek often uses two interrogatives in the same sentence to ask two questions at once. For the construction of the question, see on 492; for tmesis of the verb, see on 80.

585 Ἔννοσι: voc. < ἔνοσις, literally, "shaking, quaking."

589 ἀνά: here, "throughout."

591 λάινα: "of stone, marble."
κίοσιν < κίων, ονος, ὁ or ἡ, "column."

592 διάδρομα: literally, "running asunder."

594 αἴθοπα < αἴθωψ, οπος, "fiery, flashing."

596 λεύσσεις: "see, behold."

599 κεραυνόβολος: "the thunderstruck one," i.e., Semele; for the relative clause, see the last three lines of D's note on 596-599.

600 δίκετε: "throw, cast."
τρομερά: "trembling."

The Stranger's Narrative

604 ἐκπεπληγμέναι < ἐκπλήσσω, "strike out (of one's senses), amaze, astound."

607 σαρκός < σάρξ, σαρκός ἡ, "flesh, body."
ἐξαμείψασαι: fem. part. < ἐξαμείβω, "change."

611 σκοτεινάς: "dark."

615 συνῆψε: aor. < συνάπτω, "bind together."
βρόχοις: See on 545.

616 καθύβρισ(α): literally, "I insulted."
617 ἡμῶν: In tragedy, individuals often use 1st pl. when referring to themselves. See S 1008.
618 οὗ: here, "where"; see S 1448.
      πρός φάτναις: "at the feeding trough."
      καθεῖρξ(ε): "shut in, confined"; cf. on 443.
619 τῷδε ... γόνασι καὶ χηλαῖς ποδῶν: "(around) him (the bull), ... the knees and hooves of his feet"; for the partitive appositive with the construction of whole and part, see S 985. Although the object (τῷδε) of περί precedes the preposition, there is no anastrophe of the accent because, as D points out, this is a case of tmesis of the verb περιβάλλω.
620 ἱδρῶτα: "sweat."
621 χείλεσιν < χεῖλος, ους, τό, "lip."
622 θάσσων: "sitting."
624 ἀνῆψ(ε) < ἀνάπτω, "light up".
      ὃ δ': For the article as demonstrative, see S 1106; δέ often indicates change in subject.
      αἴθεσθαι: "to be ablaze."
625 ᾖσσ(ε): See on 147; here intransitive, "dart, move quickly."
      ἐκεῖσε κᾆτ' ἐκεῖσε: literally, "in that direction and then in that direction." κᾆτ' = καὶ εἶτα.
      δμωσίν < δμώς, ωός, ὁ, "slave."
626 ἐννέπων: "telling, bidding."
627 διαμεθείς: "leaving, giving up."
      μόχθον: "toil, trouble."
628 ἵεται: See on 139.
631 κἀκέντει = καὶ ἐκέντει, "and he was stabbing."
633 ἔρρηξεν: See on 292.
      χαμᾶζε: "to the ground."
634 ἰδόντι: literally, "for him having seen."
638 ψοφεῖ γοῦν ἀρβύλη: literally, "at any rate, a shoe makes a noise."
639 προνώπι(α): "the area in front of the facade."
641 πρός: "characteristic of," as often with gen.
      ἀσκεῖν: See on 476.
647 στῆσον πόδ(α): literally, "stay your foot."
652 D prefers to give this line to Pentheus as a direct response to Dionysos in 651. τοῦτο is an internal acc.: "This is a reproach, in fact, you make to Dionysos, a pretty one." D gives line 653 to Pentheus as well, believing that something has been lost between the two lines rather than before them, probably saying that Dionysos is in the city and that Pentheus has violent intentions against him.
653 κλῄειν: "to shut, lock."
655 πλὴν ἅ = πλὴν τούτων ἅ, "except for (these things,) the things in respect to which."
659 φευξούμεθα = φευξόμεθα, often in Euripides and comedy.

665 οἴστροισι λευκὸν κῶλον ἐξηκόντισαν: literally, "with stings they shot out their white limb."
668 παρρησίᾳ: "openness, frankness."
669 στειλώμεθα < στέλλω, here, "check, repress." For the use of 1st pl., see on 617.
671 τοὐξύθυμον = τὸ ὀξύθυμον, "sharp-temperedness."
672 ἀθῷος: "unpunished, unharmed."
675 τὸν ὑποθέντα: "the one having suggested."
677 λέπας: neut. acc., "rock, crag."
679 ἀκτῖνας: "rays."
683 ηὗδον < εὕδω, "sleep."
       παρειμέναι: perf. part. < παρίημι, "relax."
684 ἐρείσασαι: aor. part. < ἐρείδω, "(make to) lean, press against."
       φόβην: "hair."
686 εἰκῇ: "at random."
687 ψόφῳ: "noise"; cf. on 638.
688 ἠρημωμένας: perf. part. < ἐρημόω, "abandon, isolate."
689 ὠλόλυξεν < ὀλολύζω, "cry to the gods, cry aloud."
690 δέμας: "body."
691 μυκήμα(τα): "roars, bellowings."
693 ἀνῇξαν: aor. < ἀναΐσσω, "start up"; see on 147.
695 κόμας < κόμη, "hair."
696f ἀμμάτων σύνδεσμ(α): "bonds of the sashes/girdles."
698 ὄφεσι < ὄφις, ὄφεως, ἡ, "snake."
       κατεζώσαντο < καταζώννυμι, "gird fast, gird oneself."
       λιχμῶσιν < λιχμάω, "lick."
699 ἀγκάλαισι: "in their bent arms."
       δορκάδ(α) < δορκάς, άδος, ἡ, "deer."
       σκύμνους: "cubs, pups."
701 νεοτόκοις: "having just given birth."
       σπαργῶν < σπαργάω, "be full, swell."
704 ἔπαισεν < παίω, "strike."
705 δροσώδης < δροσώδης, ες, "dewy."
       νοτίς: "moisture."
709 διαμῶσαι: part. < διαμάω, "cut through, scrape away."
715 ἔριν < ἔρις, ιδος, ἡ, "strife," here, "disputation, discourse."
722 θάμνων: "bushes."
       φόβαις: here, "foliage"; see on 684.
728 θρῴσκουσα: "leaping, springing."
729 'ξεπήδησ' = ἐξεπήδησα, "I leaped out."
730 λόχμην: "thicket."
734 ἐξηλύξαμεν < ἐξαλύσκω, "escape."
735 σπαραγμόν: "ritual dismemberment."
       νεμομέναις: "grazing, feeding," with μόσχοις in 736, "young heifers."

737   ἄν: here, and in 740, producing the sense of the apodosis of a past contrary to fact condition with understood protasis, "If you had been there, ... "
      εὔθηλον πόριν: "a young heifer with distended udder."
738   μυκωμένην: "bellowing"; cf. on 691.
739   δαμάλας: "mature heifers."
      διεφόρουν < διαφορέω, "tear in pieces."
740   πλεύρ(α): "ribs, side."
      δίχηλον ἔμβασιν: literally, "cloven-footed tread."
741   κρεμαστά: "hung up."
742   ἀναπεφυρμέν(α) < ἀναφύρω, "defile."
743   κἀς = καὶ εἰς.
747   κόραις: "pupils."
750   στάχυν: See on 264.
752   νέρθεν: "beneath, below."
754   διέφερον: here, "pillaged."
755f D points out that ὁπόσα probably includes both the children they kidnapped and the objects they pillaged. χαλκός and σίδηρος refer to household utensils rather than weapons. However, he is unhappy with the text and believes something may be lost after 756.
758   βοστρύχοις: See on 493.
760   οὗπερ: "at which very point."
761   τοῖς μέν: D prefers τὰς μέν, which would be the object of ἤμασσε, "made bloody."
      λογχωτόν: "lance-headed."
763   κἀπενώτιζον = καὶ ἀπενώτιζον (< ἀπονωτίζω), "make (someone) turn his back."
767f σταγόνα δ' ἐκ παρηίδων ... ἐξεφαίδρυνον χροός: "cleared away the drop from the skin of her cheeks."
782   ἀπαντᾶν < ἀπαντάω, "to meet (me here)."
784   ψάλλουσι νευράς: "pluck the bowstring."

Scene 3

789   οὔ φημι χρῆναί σ': "I deny that you ought to," i.e., "I say that you ought not."
792f οὐ μὴ φρενώσεις ... σώσῃ: For the imperative force of future interrogatives, see on 254. φρενώσεις < φρενόω, "teach, instruct."
797   πτυχαῖς: "folds," i.e., "glades."
804   δίχα: "apart from," + gen..
812   σταθμόν: "weight."
819   κἀπιχειρήσεις = καὶ ἐπιχειρήσεις.
821   στεῖλαι: aor. mid. imperative < στέλλω, here, "put on."
      χρωτί: dat. sing.; see on 24.
823   μή: introduces a purpose clause; see S 2193.
825   ἐξεμούσωσεν < ἐκμουσόω, "teach thoroughly."
827   στελῶ: See on 821; here, "equip."

16 Euripides' *Bacchae*

μολῶν: See on 553.
828 στολήν: "apparel."
831 ταναόν: "long."
ἐκτενῶ < ἐκτείνω, "stretch out."
833 ποδήρεις: "reaching the feet, floor-length."
836 ἐνδῦναι: 2nd aor. inf. < ἐνδύω, "put on (clothing)."
838 κατασκοπήν: "reconnaissance."
842 'γγελᾶν = ἐγγελᾶν < ἐγγελάω, "mock, laugh at."
843 ἄν = ἃ ἄν.
844 πάρα: with this accentuation = πάρεστι, "is present."
847 δώσει δίκην: See on 489. For the gen. of the crime with cognate acc., see S 1377.
849 πρόσω: See on 392.
850 τεισώμεθ(α): aor. mid. subj. < τίνω, "punish."
ἔκστησον < ἐξίστημι; sc. αὐτόν as object.
852 οὐ μὴ θελήσῃ: For οὐ μή + aor. subj. expressing emphatic denial, see S 1804.
853 τοῦ φρονεῖν: governed by ἔξω.
854 ὀφλεῖν: 2nd aor. < ὀφλισκάνω, "bring on oneself, incur as a penalty."
856 ἀπειλῶν: "boasts, threats."
857 κόσμον: here, "costume," obj. of προσάψων < προσάπτω, "attach, apply," in 859.
858 κατσφαγείς: aor. pass. part. < κατασφάζω, "murder."
860 ἐν τέλει: "in authority."
861 ἠπίωτατος: "most gentle, most kind."

Stasimon 3

863 ἆρ(α): Because ἆρα in this position usually introduces a question, D believes that a question mark should be added either after ῥίπτουσ' in 865 or after κυνῶν in 872.
864 δέραν: "neck."
865 δροσερόν: "dewy."
866 χλοεραῖς = χλωραῖς, "green."
867 λείμακος < λεῖμαξ, λείμακος, ἡ, "meadow."
869 θήραν < θήρα, θήρας, ἡ, "hunt."
φυλακᾶς < φυλακή, ῆς, ἡ, "watch, guard."
871 θωύσσων < θωύσσω, "buzz, call, shout."
κυναγέτας = κυναγέτης, "hunter."
872 συντείνῃ δράμημα κυνῶν: literally, "stretches together the run of his dogs."
873 μόχθοις: See on 627.
876 ἔρνεσιν: "young shoots."
878 γέρας < γέρας, γέρως, τό, "honor."
880 κρείσσω: acc. sing.

881 ὅ τι καλὸν φίλον ἀεί: literally, "whatever is good (morally) is always dear."

882 μόλις: "with painful effort," here, "grudgingly."

884 ἀπευθύνει: "make straight, correct."

888f κρυπτεύουσι δὲ ποικίλως δαρὸν χρόνου πόδα: literally, "but they conceal intricately the long foot of time."

893 δαπάνα: "expense."

895f Although there are several possible ways to construe these lines, as D points out, he considers it best to read the τ' as connecting these lines to the preceding lines as another acc.-inf. construction with νομίζειν; sc. εἶναι with τὸ ... νόμιμον as subj. and ἀεὶ φύσει τε πεφυκός as a compound pred.

903 χεῖμα: neuter singular, "winter storm."
       ἔκιχεν < κιχάνω, "reach, come upon."

905f ἑτέρᾳ δ' ἕτερος ἕτερον ὄλβῳ καὶ δυνάμει παρῆλθεν: "One man surpasses one man in one way, another another in another way, in happiness and power."

Scene 4

913 ἀσπούδαστα: "(things) not to be pursued."

923 ὁμαρτεῖ < ὁμαρτέω, "accompany, attend," + dat.
       ὤν: concessive.

925f οὐχὶ τὴν Ἰνοῦς στάσιν ἢ τὴν Ἀγαύης ἑστάναι: literally, "(Do I not appear) to stand the stance of Ino or Agaue?"

929 καθήρμοσα < καθαρμόζω, "adjust."

931 μεθώρμισα < μεθορμίζω, "remove from an anchorage."

933 ὄρθου: imperative.

942 εἰκασθήσομαι: fut. pass. < εἰκάζω, "liken."

946 αὐταῖσι βάκχαις τοῖς ἐμοῖς ὤμοις: dat. of accompaniment followed by instrumental dat (S 1507), "Bacchae and all with my shoulders." For the use of the dat. of accompaninent with αὐτός in describing destruction, see S 1525.

949 ἀνασπάσω: aor. subj. < ἀνασπάω, "pry up."

950 βραχίονα < βραχίων, ονος, ὁ, "arm."

955 Literally, "You will be hidden the hiding which it is necessary for you to be hidden." For acc. retained with a passive verb, see S 1747.

969 τρυφᾶν < τρυφάω, "live luxuriously, be licentious."

970 ἅπτομαι: here, "take part, participate."

973 ἔκτειν(ε): imperative < ἐκτείνω, "stretch out."

Stasimon 4

979 ἀνοιστρήσατε: See on 32.

981 λυσσώδη < λυσσώδης, ες, "raging, frantic."

984 ἀπύσει < ἠπύω, "call, shout."

994 λαιμῶν < λαιμός, οῦ, ὁ, "throat."

1002 γνωμᾶν: Doric gen. pl.
      σωφρόνα: nom. sing. D prefers σωφρόνισμα, "corrective."
1002f ἀπροφάσιστος ἐς τὰ θεῶν ἔφυ· βροτείως τ᾽ ἔχειν: D
      prefers to place the semicolon after θάνατος and suggests reading
      ἀπροφασίστως instead of ἀπροφάσιστος. The τ᾽ in line 1004 links
      the two adverbs, which are both taken with ἔχειν as the subject of ἔφυ.
1006f D's preferred solution to the textual difficulties in this line is to read
      χαίρω θηρεύουσα τάδ᾽ ἕτερα μεγάλα φανερὰ τ᾽ ὄντ᾽· ἄγει δ᾽ ἐπὶ
      τὰ καλὰ βίον, "I enjoy hunting these other things, being great and
      apparent; and they lead life to the good."
1007 νάει⟨ν⟩ < νάω, "flow." ⟨ ⟩ enclose material which the editor
      believes was originally present in the text.
1022 ἀγέλαν < ἀγέλη, "herd."

Scene 5

1028 This line, which makes little sense here, has been interpolated from
      Euripides' *Medea*, as D notes.
1034 μέλεσι: here, "songs."
1035 πτήσσω: "crouch in fear, cower."
1036 D's note includes what he believes is missing in this lacuna.
1042 ἐκπορίζων: "contriving."
1043 θεράπνας: "dwellings."
1048 ποιηρόν: "grassy."
1056 ἐκλιποῦσαι ... ὡς: For postpositive ὡς introducing a simile, see
      S 3002.
1061 ἀμβάς < ἀναβαίνω.
1063 τοὐντεῦθεν = τὸ ἐντεῦθεν; adv.
1069 ἔκαμπτεν < κάμπτω, "bend."
1070 ὄζων: "boughs, branches."
1072 ἀναχαιτίσειε < ἀναχαιτίζω, "toss (the mane), unseat."
1073 ἐστηρίζετο: literally, "was established."
1076 θάσσων: "sitting."
1078 ὡς μὲν εἰκάσαι: "to make a guess, as one would guess."
1080 τἀμά = τὰ ἐμά.
1081 γέλων: See on 250.
      τιθέμενον: with two acc.'s, "making x (be) y"; cf. on 11.
      τιμωρεῖσθε: "punish, exact vengeance from."
1084 ὕλιμος: "wooded," a two-termination adj.
1086 ὠσίν < οὖς, ὠτός, τό, "ear."
      ἠχήν: "noise."
1087 διήνεγκαν κόρας: literally, "turned their pupils in different
      directions."
1090 ᾖξαν < ἀίσσω; see on 147.
      πελείας ὠκύτητ(α): gen. of comparison and acc. of respect;
      "(not less) than a dove with respect to swiftness."

1091f Lines 1091 and 1092 are problematic and make little sense; D believes they should be left out, since they do not appear in an early papyrus text of the play.

1094 ἀγμῶν: "crags."

ἐμμανεῖς < ἐμμανής, ές, "maddened, frantic."

1096 αὐτοῦ: Pentheus. For the gen. used for the goal of a verb meaning "to aim", see S 1349.

χερμάδας κραταιβόλους: "boulders hurled with violence."

1100 ἤνυτον < ἀνύτω, a rare variant of ἀνύω, "accomplish."

1101 ὕψος < ὕψος, ους, τό, "height."

1102 λελημμένος < λαμβάνω.

1103 τέλος: adv., "at last."

1104 ῥίζας < ῥίζα, ης, ἡ, "root."

ἀνεσπάρασσον < ἀνασπαράσσω, "tear up."

1110 κἀξανέσπασαν = καὶ ἐξανέσπασαν < ἐξανασπάω, "tear up and away from."

1111 χαμαιριφής: "hurled to the ground"

1112 οὖδας < οὖδας, ους, τό, "earth."

1114 ἱερέα: nom., "priestess."

1122 ἀφρόν: "foam, frothy blood."

1124 ἐκ Βακχίου κατείχετ(ο): "she was possessed by Bacchus."

1128 εὐμάρειαν: "dexterity."

1129 θἀτέρῳ = τὰ ἕτερα, "the other (side of the body)."

1131 πᾶσ' ὁμοῦ βοή: "every cry together."

1134 ἴχνος αὐταῖς ἀρβύλαις: "foot with boots and all"; see on 946.

1136 διεσφαίριζε: literally, "threw about like a ball."

1137 στύφλοις: "hard, rough."

1141 πήξασ(α) < πήγνυμι, "make fast, affix."

1144 γαυρουμένη: "exulting in, priding herself on."

1152 χρωμένοις: "making use (of it)."

Stasimon 5

1155 ἐκγενέτα: "offspring"; for the Doric gen. sing., see S 214 D5.

1163f χέρ' αἵματι στάζουσαν περιβαλεῖν: inf. in apposition to καλὸς αγών with acc. direct object.

1166 ἐν διαστρόφοις ὄσσοις: "in (a state of) distorted eyes."

Exodos

1173 ἔμαρψα < μάρπτω, "catch, seize."

1174 ἶνιν < ἶνις, ὁ, "son."

1175 πάρα: See on 844; here, "it is possible."

1176 ἐρημίας: "in the wilderness"; for the chorographic gen., see S 1311.

1177 Κιθαιρών: nom.

1178 κατεφόνευσε: Subject is Kithairon.

1181 ἄλλα = ἄλλη.

1182 τί Κάδμου;: "Why (do you say) 'of Kadmos'?"
1183 ἔθιγε: here, "stuck"; see on 304.
D does not believe any lines have been lost here.
1184 θοίνας: "feast," gen. with μετέχω, "share in."
μετέχω: deliberative subjunctive.
1188 ὥστε = ὥσπερ.
1190 ἀνέπηλ(ε): aor. < ἀναπάλλω, here, "urge on, set in motion."
1197 ἀγάλλῃ < ἀγάλλομαι, "exult, take delight."
γέγηθα < γηθέω, "rejoice"; perf. has pres. sense.
1206 δικτύοισιν: "hunting nets."
1208 λογχοποιῶν < λογχοποιός, "spear-maker."
1213 προσαμβάσεις: acc. pl. < προσάμβασις, "ascent, going up."
1214 πασσαλεύσῃ < πασσαλεύω, "attach by pegs, fasten to," + dat.
1218 μοχθῶν < μοχθέω, "be weary, distressed."
1220 ταὐτῷ = τῷ αὐτῷ.
1225 κάμψας < κάμπτω, here, "return"; cf. 1069.
1229 δρυμούς < δρυμός, "wood, thicket." D prefers to read the dative,
δρυμοῖς.
οἰστροπλῆγας < οἰστροπλήξ, ῆγος, "stung by a gadfly, driven
wild."
1235 ἐξόχως: "especially, outstandingly."
1236 κερκίδας: "shuttles."
1238 ὠλέναισιν: "hands, arms from the elbow down."
1239 τἀριστεῖα = τὰ ἀριστεῖα, "the prize."
1240 ἀγκρεμασθῇ < ἀνακρεμάννυμι, "hang up as a dedication."
1248 κακῶν ... σῶν: For the gen. of the cause, see S 1407.
1252 σκυθρωπόν: "sullen, angry-looking."
1255 ὀριγνῷτ(ο): opt. < ὀριγνάομαι, literally, "stretch after, reach for,
grasp at."
1256 νουθετητέος: "he must be admonished." For the personal (passive)
construction with a verbal adj., see S 2151.
1257 σούστιν = σοί ἐστίν.
1265 ἐξυπεῖπας < *ἐξυπολέγω, "advise."
1266 αὐτός = ὁ αὐτός; sc. εἶναι.
1267 διειπετέστερος: "more translucent" (D).
1268 πτοηθέν: "distraction"; aor. pass. part. < πτοέω, "excite, scare."
1270 ἔννους = ἔννοος, nom. sing.
1271 κἀποκρίναι' = καὶ ἀποκρίναιο.
1272 ἐκλέλησμαι < ἐκλανθάνομαι, "forget."
1276 ἐμῇ = ἐμοῦ.
1277 ἀγκάλαις: See on 699.
1280 ἔα: a gasp.
1283 μῶν: introduces a question which expects a negative answer.
1285 ᾠμωγμένον < οἰμώζω, "lament."
1287 δύστην(ε) ἀλήθει(α): vocative.
1288 πήδημ' ἔχει: literally, "has a leap," i.e., "fears"; with τὸ μέλλον.
as object.

1289   **κατέκτας**: 2nd aor. < κατακτείνω.
       σέθεν = σοῦ.
1294   **κατήραμεν**: aor. < καταίρω, "swoop down."
1299   **μόλις**: See on 882.
1300   **συγκεκλημένον** < συγκλήω, "link."
       According to D, at least three lines are missing here, in which Agaue's
       question is answered, most likely in the negative, but it is uncertain
       what else occurred in this lacuna.
1303   **συνῆψε**: subject is ὁ θεός.
1305   **ὅστις**: "as being one who."
1307   **κατθανόν(τα)**: antecedent is τόδ' ἔρνος in 1304. Although they
       do not agree in gender, both refer to Pentheus; see S 1013.
1308   **ὦ τέκνον**: addresses Pentheus.
1309   **τοὐμὸν μέλαθρον**: As a parallel, D quotes line 57 of Euripides'
       Iphigeneia at Tauris, "For male children are the pillars of houses."
1313   **ἐκβεβλήσομαι**: fut. perf. < ἐκβάλλω.
1315   **κἀξήμησα** = καὶ ἐξήμησα; < ἐξαμάω, "reap."
       θέρος: "summer, harvest."
1319   **προσπτύξῃ** < προσπτύσσω, "embrace."
1322   **κολάζω**: subj., "chastise."
1325   **ὑπερφρονεῖ**: "looks down on, despises," + gen.
1329f For an account of what probably takes place in this lacuna, see D, pp.
       234-235.
1331   **ὄφεος**: poetic. gen. < ὄφις, "snake."
       ἀλλάξει: See on 53.
1335   **πέρσεις** < πέρθω, "sack, destroy."
1337   **διαρπάσωσι** < διαρπάζω, "plunder."
1339   **καθιδρύσει**: "will establish, consecrate."
1349   **ἐπένευσεν** < ἐπινεύω, "give the nod to, approve, sanction."
1350   **δέδοκται**: used in decrees, "it is resolved."
1351   **μέλλε(τε)**: here, "delay, hesitate."
1361   **καταιβάτην**: "downward plunging" (D).
1363   **στερεῖσα**: aor. pass. part. < στερέω, "deprive."
1365   Literally, "as a swan bird (embrace) a white drone."
1367   **ἐπίκουρος**: "ally, assistance."
1371   As D points out, this sentence is incomplete and its meaning is
       unknown.
1378   **ἀγέραστον**: "without honor."
1380   **τόδ(ε)**: refers to χαίρειν in 1379 in its idiomatic sense of leave-
       taking, and in its literal sense, "enjoy," which is contrasted with
       χαλεπῶς.
1386   **ὅθι** = οὗ, "where."
1391   **πόρον** < πόρος, ὁ, "path."